MODELLING WWII FIGURES

Osprey Modelling Manuals
Volume 9

Publication Manager: Rodrigo Hernandez Cabos

Series Editor: Jerry Scutts

OSPREY

Osprey Modelling Manuals 9

MODELLING WWII FIGURES

First published in Great Britain in 2000 by Osprey Publishing, Elms Court, Chapel Way, Botley, Oxford OX2 9LP, United Kingdom.
Email: info@ospreypublishing.com

© Accion Press, S. A., C/Ezequiel Solana, 16, 28017, Madrid, Spain. Euromodelismo. Depósito Legal M-19729-1992

ISBN 1 84176 137 0

English edition packaged by Compendium, 1st Floor, 43 Frith Street, London, W1V 5TE

00 01 02 03 04 10 9 8 7 6 5 4 3 2 1

Publication Manager: Rodrigo Hernández Cabos
Photographs: Antonio Soler García, Salvador Gómez Mico, Rodrigo Hernández Cabos
Modelling Team: Aitor Azcue Gracia, Luis Gómez Platón, Ismael Rivas Rodriguez, Jesús Pérez Huelamo, Miguel Felipe Carrascal.

Printed in Spain

For a catalogue of all books published by Osprey Military, Automotive and Aviation please contact:

**The Marketing Manager, Osprey Direct UK, PO Box 140, Wellingborough, Northants, NN8 4ZA, United Kingdom. Tel. (0)1933 443863, Fax (0)1933 443849.
Email: info@ospreydirect.co.uk**

The Marketing Manager, Osprey Direct USA, PO Box 130. Sterling Heights, MI 48311-0130, USA. Tel. 248 399 6191, Fax 248 399 6194. Email: info@ospreydirectusa.com

Visit Osprey at:
www.ospreypublishing.com

Warfare in the 20th century, with its khaki battledress and green and brown camouflage patterns, is much less interesting visually than the bright uniforms and colourful insignia of the past — think of the Napoleonic or Roman period. However, such a small colour range means that painting World War II figures realistically is a subtle art and one that — if performed well — will make a real difference to your models. This book provides tips and pointers on a selection of subjects ranging from the heat of the Western Desert to the snows of the Arctic north, from the years of Blitzkrieg to the final days of the Third Reich.

BRITISH INFANTRYMAN

This scene shows a typical British soldier of World War II. He's wearing the characteristic British battledress and Pattern 1937 webbing, including a small pack, an entrenching tool, water bottle in container on right hip and bayonet on left, webbing gaiters, a Lee Enfield No. 4 rifle, and a Mk 1 steel helmet covered with helmet netting. Note the capacious map pocket on the left thigh and the black bull on the yellow background on his left shoulder. This is the insignia of 11th Armoured Division, so it is likely that this infantryman belongs to the division's motorized infantry brigade.

The pieces that make up this Hornet figure are well finished. The backpack and equipment are modelled from a single piece that fits perfectly into a cavity found in the back, thus reducing the amount of metal used for the figure. The sculpting work is excellent, and the rendering of the facial features is outstanding as is so much of Roger Saunders' work. Citadel pigments were used to paint the figure; these pigments are high quality acrylic paints, sold in small plastic containers, and offering an extensive range of bright colours, primarily intended for use in the painting of fantasy miniatures (which accounts for the unusual names for the military modeller!).

The base colour was obtained by mixing snake-bite leather, bestial brown, hobgoblin orange and bleached bone. Add a bit of grey to the mix in order to reduce the brightness of the colour. To lighten, add white to the base colour; to darken, add chaos black and blood angel orange. The holsters and belts were painted by combining the base colour with a bit of white and the darkened base mix; lighting effects for this area can be obtained by adding more white to this mix. The flesh colour was a combination of snake-bite leather, terracotta and blood angel orange. The proportions of this mix will vary depending on the desired skin tone. Lighten the flesh colour by adding white, and darken by adding terracotta.

The corner of the building and ground surface were made from 0.45mm thick balsawood, over the top of which a layer of grey tones and white using a dry brush, and finish by applying dark brown and black washes.

The figure was painted with Citadel paints.

The quality of the figure is excellent, with an outstanding rendering of facial features.

The corner of the building was built using balsawood and Milliput.

The uniform and equipment are painted using brown tones, subsequently adding white and black to lighten and darken.

Milliput was applied to render the brick texture. The bullet holes were made using the edge of a blade. The same system was used to make the paving stones. To paint the scene, apply various

5

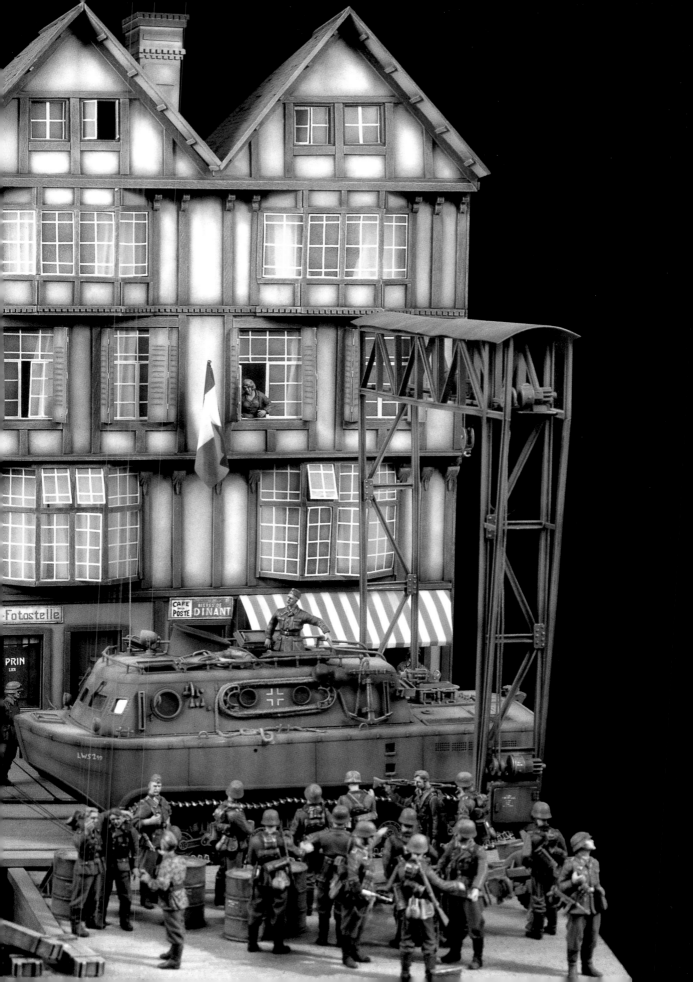

CALAIS 1940 — Operation 'Sealion'

Once Hitler had conquered France and the Low Countries, his next objective — as outlined in War Directive No 16 of 16 July 1940 — was the invasion of England. The plan was codenamed Operation *'Seelöwe'* (Sealion).

Background figures and details of secondary importance are often used to fill otherwise empty areas to add interest and depth in this type of composition.

The invasion of Britain was predicated on two main events: the defeat of the Royal Air Force to ensure that the skies above the invasion force were clear of British aircraft, and the blocking of the Channel to the Royal Navy. Once those aims had been achieved, the first German wave — some nine divisions — would land between Worthing in Sussex and Dover, across from Calais in Kent. Subsequently a second and third wave would follow up once the bridgehead was secured.

As we know today, Goering's Luftwaffe did not clear the skies of the RAF: far from it, his air forces received a bloody nose in the autumn of 1940. Indeed, RAF bombers were able to strike against the invasion fleet all over northern Europe where it gathered in harbours and ports. By October Hitler's attentions were turning eastwards; by January 1941, the fleet was dispersed.

But for a few months in 1940 it seemed not so much a case of whether the invasion would take place, but simply when and where . . .

The decoration of the façade is an important element of the building as it adds a great deal of realism; happily this often consists of simple elements that are easy to paint.

DIORAMA

This scene is of Calais harbour, the closest French port to the south coast of England, and shows one of the many invasion exercises that took place in 1940. German units load onto an old passenger ferry converted into a troopship — note the anti-aircraft emplacement. One of the amphibious vehicles that will be needed to transfer troops from ship to shore is being loaded onto the ship, watched by heavily armed troops.

BUILDINGS

The first step is to organise the space for the diorama. Choose the vehicles you want to use — they serve as the focal point around which the event can be created. Here, the buildings were made using lightweight card, on a base made from a 61 x 51cm piece of chipboard. Once the framework is complete, start to cover the structure with suitably textured plastic sheet; for example, where a stone effect is needed, cover the framework with sheets of the required texture — or you can achieve the same results by applying and carving plaster. A variety of sandpapers can also be used for this job — different thicknesses are used to represent different types of surface.

The next stage is to add fine detailing to perfect the building. The strips of wood are the same material that was used to cover the ship; the shutters (with

To create an eye-catching and dynamic façade, think about adding a good variety of colours and plenty of details, including figures.

9

The second important group of figures occupies a deck on the ferry.

wooden streaks) are engraved plastic sheets with stretched plastic used for the hinges. The windows are made from acetate, and the window frames outlined by the careful application of black and white adhesive tape (a variety of thicknesses and colours can be found in art shops).

The 'fish scale' finish used for the roof is achieved by punching holes in thick sheets of paper (the type used for folders in ring binders). The paper circles left over after the hole-punching can be used as roof tiles — these can be glued in place. Building the roof is a tedious task but the result is well worth the effort.

The construction of the pier requires a layer of plastic sheets, similar to the covering of the building. The water is formed by using Das Pronto modelling clay, which is then painted with Humbrol green and sealed with several layers of varnish.

Painting the building is in several phases. The first involves the use of an airbrush and Humbrol paints; apply dark tones such as greys and greens and subsequently make the surface lighter by applying successively lighter tones. Once this is completed, make specific areas stand out by using a dry brush. Finally, use coloured pastel crayons (particularly browns, oranges and greens) to give the effect of grime and damp.

This part of the harbour stands out with finely finished houses and a group of motorcycles.

VEHICLES AND MODELS

CRANE Made from plastic sheet and strips of wood, the pictorial reference for this came from a railway model. The paints are the same as those used for the buildings.

FERRY Build a boat-shaped structure out of lightweight card, then cover it with plastic sheet. Use the same sheeting for the doors and cranes. The deck is made from strips of wood; the vertical railing is of brass, also used for other ship details; the horizontal railings are made from spaghetti, and the cargo door cables are plastic.

SdKfz222 This is an old Tamiya model with minor details added, the most interesting of which is the frame antenna.

AMPHIBIOUS VEHICLE A Mini-Art resin model was used but unfortunately it did not fit together very well — the wheel assembly was out of place, and so the wheels seem to be far too close to one another.

MOTORCYCLES These are Italeri and Tamiya kits which were assembled, painted and then had considerable quantities of personal gear added.

The SdKfz222 is found in the least obvious area of the diorama — the part of the harbour which is partially covered by the ferry.

One side of the diorama is covered by buildings, formed and shaped using lightweight card. The details of each building are created by using a combination of plaster, plastic and wood.

ANTI-AIRCRAFT WEAPONS
These are familiar models by Tamiya to which minor details have been added. The cannon have been painted in different

FIGURES

tones of green and brown to give the impression that the ship carries a variety of weapons. The painting and aging process is achieved by using the same techniques as in the rest of the diorama.

ANTI AIRCRAFT-TRAILER This is also a Tamiya model, but with no modifications.

There are over 50 figures in this diorama. They come from a number of manufacturers, mainly Verlinden and Hornet . When creating a diorama with this many figures, it is worthwhile — and a lot cheaper — to make a silicone-rubber mould of an original figure and mass-produce the others. If you do this, remove the limbs from the

The centre of attention focuses on this varied group of figures.

figure you chose. This allows for more flexibility of anatomical positioning once the arms and legs are reattached. Cast the replica figures in lead or tin, with the latter being the better as it takes a crisper casting.

The uniforms for the ground troops were painted using greys for the trousers and greens for the jackets. All the paints used were Humbrol. These soldiers are from the Grossdeutschland Motorised Infantry Regiment, so suitable cuffbands and shoulder straps have been added.

After the fall of France, Grossdeutschland spent August to October 1940 training for Operation *'Seelöwe'*; after this November and December was spent training for Operation 'Felix' — the projected invasion of Gibraltar.

This diorama was awarded a bronze medal (category 15) at Euromilitaire '96.

This vehicle was assembled from a Mini-Art resin kit.

AFRIKA KORPS
German Troops in the Desert

and air cover, advancing some 50 miles to Sidi Barrani. There they remained until Operation 'Compass', which saw the British forces first push back the invaders and then destroy the retreating Italian Army at Beda Fomm.

Hitler, alarmed by the Italian defeat, decided to send German reinforcements to North Africa in the shape of the 5th Light Division (later renamed the 21st Panzer Division) and the 15th Panzer Division. These units formed the Deutsches Afrika Korps under the command of Generalleutnant Erwin Rommel, who had already proved his worth during the invasion of France.

The Afrika Korps suffered a number of handicaps that left it short of soldiers, supplies and material. To begin with, all its reinforcements had to come

The exact position of the holster will need to be worked out and the leg will require stretching.

In 1941 the first detachments arrived in Libya of what would eventually become one of the most famous units of World War II — the fearsome Deutsches Afrika Korps.

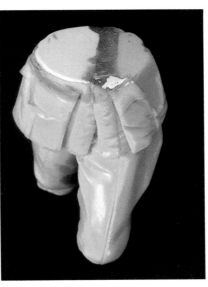

To correct the angle of the upper body, a small wedge of plastic card can be inserted in the waist area.

When Italy declared war on Great Britain in June 1940, troops from the two countries confronted each other in the Western Desert of North Africa, across the Libya-Egypt border. The Italians attacked Egypt on 13 September 1940, with a sizeable army

The base colour should completely cover the surface.

Once the effects of light and shade are completed, outline the seams on the trousers.

the Caucasus. However, Rommel's talents were recognised and he would be promoted Generalfeldmarschall in 1942. He would leave the theatre a sick man in March 1943, relocating to North-West Europe to control the defence of France against invasion. He would die at his own hand following implication in the July 1944 Bomb Plot, the attempted assassination of Hitler.

Even today, the memory of the 'Desert Fox' and the Afrika Korps remain synonymous with bravery and sacrifice, their image a permanent reminder of the desert war.

ASSEMBLY AND PAINTING

This resin figure is 120mm high, and is made by the British firm Mil-Art (ref. 120/3 MG34 Machine Gunner; Afrika Korps).

The figure is well proportioned with fine detail, the only minor quibble being the slightly exaggerated tilt of the upper body. To correct this flaw, a wedge of plastic card is inserted in the area where the legs and torso meet; then, using modelling filler, the right leg is elongated by a couple of millimetres.

across the Mediterranean and the British still held Malta, a base from which they could harass shipping. On top of this the Oberkommando der Wehrmacht (German Armed Forces High Command) gave priority to supplying their forces on the Eastern Front. However, despite the lack of resources, Rommel led a series of brilliant and powerful offensives based on

and equipment told and the Germans lost Africa. With it they lost the chance of joining up with their comrades fighting in

With a few days' growth of stubble the face gains character.

intelligent tactics and a shrewd use of armoured vehicles, which compensated in part for the numerical superiority of the British Eighth Army.

In the end, the numerical superiority of the Allies' forces

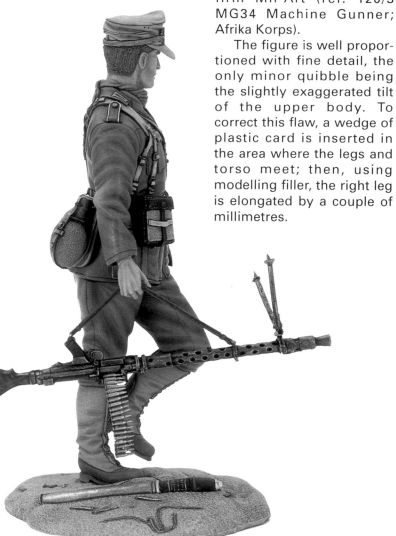

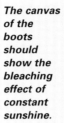

The canvas of the boots should show the bleaching effect of constant sunshine.

A satin finish is applied to imitate a leather shine.

Once all the pieces are ready and all the shaping touches completed, give the figure a preliminary coat of paint so that the resin is well covered.

As usual, the painting of the figure begins by working the areas of flesh (face and hands), which should be a browny colour to imitate a desert sun tan. To achieve this effect, carefully add a coffee-brown tone to the usual mix of flesh colours. A touch of character is implied with some stubble; this effect is achieved by carefully applying touches of a diluted green-grey tone.

The official colour of the tropical uniform designed for the Afrika Korps was olive-green. However, in African service the uniform appeared to have more of a khaki tone because it was bleached by washing and long exposure to the sun, resulting in the uniform colours taking on the tone of the desert sand. Each item of

Far Left: The colour of the army jacket is slightly different to that of the trousers, therefore providing a subtle contrast.

Left: A finished version of the army jacket with the belts and details completed.

This MG34 machine gun was painted with Tamiya metallic enamels.

The ammunition belt is made of metal, allowing for flexible movement and easy gripping.

clothing has been painted in a different colour to show varying degrees of wear and damage. The tone of the trousers is based on a mix using yellow brown (a-85), olive green (a-77) and ochre green cadmium (c-89). To lighten areas add beige or pale yellow and to add shading use touches of black. For the army jacket use ochre green cadmium as a base colour, darkening with an olive tone (b-78). The base colour is lightened using a mix of ochre green cadmium and beige.

The caps were usually the most worn-out and faded items of clothing, so they should be painted in ochre green cadmium with beige undertones (this same colour was used to lighten areas on other items of clothing).

Make sure you get the detailing of personal equipment right — particularly the way they hang.

A good outlining job is an important part of the finish, as this view shows.

It is necessary to use a variety of paints (matt, satin, metallic, etc.) in order to imitate the different types of material.

The scarf and glasses add a touch of variety against the green and khaki colour scheme.

Small details (the eagle, medals, buckles and seams) help make the figure more realistic.

The webbing was an important part of the Afrika Korps uniform. It was made of canvas, a much lighter and more comfortable material than leather. Canvas colour is obtained by mixing light brown (a-83) and beige (b-17), to which touches of dark brown and yellow are added. For highlighting add white, and to render darkened areas and shadows apply a diluted brown colour. All additional equipment pieces (gas mask, holster, etc.) are painted in their usual colours.

The tropical boots were made from canvas and leather. A green canvas colour may have a variety of tones, but the most accurate representation is achieved by adding a bit of

yellow and grey to olive green. For the leather, use dark brown (Decorfin 402), and to lighten, mix it with burnt sienna (41).

The MG34 is painted with a gunmetal base to which a drop of metallic blue is added. After darkening with a black wash, go over the entire weapon with a mix of the base colour and flat aluminium using a dry brush. The butt is painted in a brownish-red, over which wooden streaks are painted; finally, a light coat of satin varnish improves the finish.

The field glasses have been painted over with the same colour as used for the cap, but with a drop of bright orange varnish applied to each lens to replicate a reflection from the desert sun.

To paint the butt of the weapon, imitate streaks of wood and then apply a satiny varnish.

MEMPHIS BELLE

The *Memphis Belle* is one of the most famous bombers in the history of American flying. Her crew was the first in the USAAF to complete a 25-mission tour of duty and live to tell the tale. Their story was told in a wartime documentary and, more recently, in a Hollywood feature film.

Based in eastern England, the American Eighth Air Force flew its first mission of World War II in August 1942 and would pound the Reich by day until the final surrender. At first, lacking the long-range fighter escort later provided by the P-51 Mustang, the bombers suffered heavy losses — a good reason for celebration when a crew reached 25 missions.

Memphis Belle flew with 324th Squadron of Eighth Air Force's 91st Bomb Group, based at Bassingbourn. Named for

Far Left: The lifejacket and body armour straps are made from thin strips of tin.

Centre Left: Use the usual techniques for creating highlights.

Left: To make small creases stand out, apply an intermediate coat using a dry-brush technique.

COLOUR TABLE

Colour base

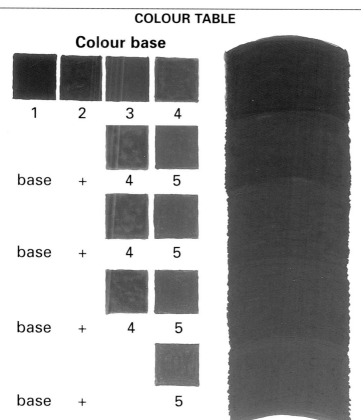

1	2	3	4

base	+	4	5

base	+	4	5

base	+	4	5

base	+		5

(Key: V = Vallejo/D = Decorfin)

Flying suit : 1. Black (V); 2. Dark brown (D); 3. Coffee brown (V); 4. Burnt sienna (D); 5. Burnt sienna (V). Dark areas and shadows: Dark brown (D) + black (V).

The chromatic gradation shown above is only a guide. The final tone will vary and will depend on the quantity of colours mixed together. The selection of the final colour will also depend on the personal taste of the painter.

The collar is darkened with a wash of brown over the cream-coloured base.

To add a little variety, paint the eyes blue.

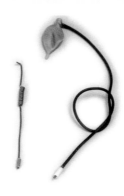

Once the leather is completed, make the zips by using aluminium colour over a black base.

Memphian Margaret Polk, pilot Robert Morgan's girl back home, *Memphis Belle*'s story was immortalised in a 1943 documentary, and the aircraft and its crew went back to the United States for a morale and fund raising tour. Rescued from the scrapheap, *Memphis Belle* was preserved and has recently been restored. It can be seen on Mud Island, Memphis.

Our model shows a B-17 crew member moments before taking off on a dangerous mission over occupied Europe. This is a Verlinden Productions figure, belonging to the 120mm resin figures series (ref 583 *Memphis Belle* B-17 Crewman).

The cable and pin can be made using copper wire and a plastic rod.

19

The variety of textures, colours and details bring realism and life to the figure.

PREPARATION AND PAINTING

With care the preparation phase should be fairly straightforward. In terms of painting, begin by working on the most important and attractive part of the figure: the flying suit. This should be relatively easy as the special texture of the garment material has been accurately simulated on the model. To make the base colour, combine matt and satin paint, mixing various tones of brown until you arrive at the colour that most accurately represents the original material (use reference information to get the full variety of colours and textures). Once the first coat is dry, render light areas in two successive applications, working in the creases. In the third application, softly apply a dry brush to highlight creases. In the final application, go over each crease individually with the brush.

Using a dry brush, add white to the cream base to highlight areas of the collar.

Wear and tear to the parachute canvas is achieved by applying areas of light beige.

Dilute the paint when making large shadows in the creases, and keep the paint thick when outlining smaller wrinkles and creases.

The boots, gloves and helmet are painted with a mix of dark

For the boots use a brown that is darker and less red than the one used for the flying suit.

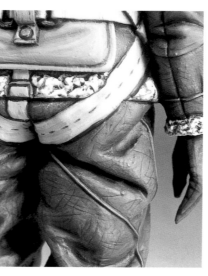

Outlining will help to define volume and separate the different items of clothing and equipment.

brown and Decorfin burnt sienna, to which a small amount of Vallejo black is added. To lighten, apply a Vallejo coffee brown. The sheepskin on the collar, cuff and waist of the bomber jacket has a cream base colour which is darkened by applying a dark brown wash. Afterwards make highlights with a dry brush using a mix of the base colour and a touch of white.

Different colours have been used to distinguish the various elements of the helmet.

This shows the full range of tones used on the figure.

The yellow of the lifejacket stands out against the brown and green colour scheme.

The lifejacket belts are painted in a different colour to the other canvas belts.

For the life jacket, mix a gold yellow cadmium with a yellow-brown colour. If necessary white can be used as a lightener, but to get a more accurate colour scheme for the life jacket a cadmium lemon is recommended.

The canvas colour of the parachute and body armour is made with an olive green and a yellowish-brown tone, to which small amounts of grey and brown are added: lighten using a beige. To achieve a degree of tonal variety, try painting the belts in slightly different colours (by adding another colour to the mix or making it lighter).

The map held by the figure was not included in the kit; a map sheet, sold separately by the manufacturer, was used.

Try to outline as many cracks and small creases as possible.

GERMAN FIGHTER PILOT

Most plastic aviation kits include a pilot or crew figure. These figures, however, are rarely of high quality and often create difficulties when you are working at a large scale.

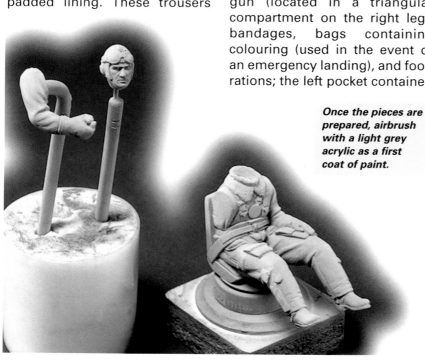

This highly detailed figure, modelled by Diego F. Fortes, is made of resin and is intended to be adaptable to the Messerschmitt Bf109G and 109E by Revell, the Focke-Wulf Fw190A by Hasegawa and the Bf109E by Matchbox, all at 1/32 scale.

The outfit is typical of those worn by German pilots during the final stages of World War II. The famous *Kanal Hoses* (channel trousers) are the most distinctive article of clothing; the name is based on the fact that these trousers were distributed among flight personnel working on operations over the English Channel in 1941.

The winter version was made out of grey-blue cotton, with a similarly coloured synthetic padded lining. These trousers also had an interior heating system, controlled by a manual thermostat that was connected to the aircraft. Distributed throughout the inside of the trousers was an assortment of emergency equipment. The large pockets over the thighs contained cartridges for the flare gun (located in a triangular compartment on the right leg), bandages, bags containing colouring (used in the event of an emergency landing), and food rations; the left pocket contained

Once the pieces are prepared, airbrush with a light grey acrylic as a first coat of paint.

the connection for the thermal system. A small yellow flag with an extendible rod was located in a lower pocket on the right leg; a survival knife was located in a similar pocket on the left leg.

When flying, pilots could wear a short, tight jacket in the Luftwaffe's grey-blue colour — the *Fliegerbluse*; most pilots, however, preferred wearing a civil or military leather jacket. The boots were black and lined with sheepskin; the legs were made of suede, and the soles of rubber. Containing several belts and zips, the boots fitted tightly around the leg. The flying helmet was made out of leather and contained a microphone to facilitate communications.

ASSEMBLY AND PAINTING

Dismembering and assembling the figure is a simple task; after ensuring that the head and right arm fit properly, both pieces are separately prepared for the paint job. Apply to both pieces a primer consisting of a Tamiya

The light areas on the jacket are a brown-red tone; the contrast between the light and dark areas must be subtle.

Next, outline the clothes and paint such details as buttons and zips.

To simulate the shiny quality of leather, apply a final coat of satin acrylic varnish.

To finish off the helmet add a satin varnish to the black area.

As a final detail, apply a shiny varnish over the lens of the glasses.

Begin decorating the sides of the leather flying helmet with a lightish brown.

The creamy-white colour of the turtle neck can be lightened by applying a little white; the fine lines of the stitching are detailed using a very dilute brown.

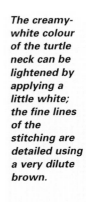

The lights and shadows of the collar are obtained by combining dry-brush and wash techniques.

Paint the parachute straps light grey and the buckles in silver.

The boots and gloves are painted in the same way as the black part of the helmet; finish with a final coat of satin varnish.

To get the seat-belt colour, mix together an olive tone with brownish-grey.

23

light grey acrylic; once dry the pieces are ready to paint.

As usual begin by painting the flesh area which, in this case, is only the face. To paint the base colour of the trousers, mix a blue (Luftwaffe 816) with small amounts of violet (960) and grey blue (943). To lighten, add light grey blue (907), and to darken add dark navy blue (898). To paint the zips, apply a mix of Adithes liquid gold and silver.

The base colour of the jacket is black (950), reduced with a small amount of brownish-grey (822). Lighten progressively with a dark leather brown (871) and a touch of leather brown (940); darken shadows by directly applying black (950). The leather collar has a brownish-beige (875) base colour, which, once dry, is darkened by washing with matt brown (984). Light effects are obtained by carefully applying a brownish-gold (877) with a dry brush.

The brown leather pieces on the sides of the flying helmet are suitable for the jacket, helmet, gloves and boots — is obtained by applying a final coat of satin varnish (852 from the Model Color acrylic range of products).

COLOUR TABLE

Trousers
Base: Luftwaffe (816) + violet (960) + bluish-grey (943)
Highlighting: Base + light bluish-grey (907)
Shading: Dark navy blue (898)

Jacket
Base: Black (950) + violet (960) + brownish-grey (822)
Highlighting: Base + dark leather brown (871) + leather brown (940)
Shading: Black (950)

Leather collar
Base: Brownish-beige (875)
Highlighting: Matt brown (984)
Shading: Gold brown (877)

Brown area of the helmet
Base: Ochre brown (856) + brownish-orange (981) + brownish-red (985)
Highlighting: Base + ochre brown (856)
Shading: Reddish brown (985)

Black area of the helmet, gloves and boots
Base: Black (950) + dark leather brown (871)
Highlighting: Base + dark leather brown (871)
Shading: Black (950)

Parachute belts
Base: Pale grey (990)
Highlighting: Base + white (951)
Shading: Neutral grey (992)

Seat belt
Base: Olive green (850) + English uniform (921)
Highlighting: Base + camouflage yellow (978)
Shading: Base + black (950)

Seat
Base: Basalt grey (869)
Highlighting: Base + mid-grey marine (870)
Shading: German grey (995)

Adithes liquid gold • Adithes liquid silver • Satin varnish (852)

painted by mixing an ochre brown (856), brownish-orange (981) and a brownish-red (985), using the ochre brown to lighten.

The black parts of the helmet, gloves and boots are painted in black (950), and highlighted with a dark leather brown (871).

The semi-glossy finish of leather —

WAFFEN SS

Painting a camouflage uniform always looks as if it will be more difficult than it really is. With careful painting, close observation and patience, the results can be excellent.

Begin by searching in magazines and books for reference material for the type of camouflage you need to replicate. Because of the large variety of troop models and styles, this research will be particularly necessary when working on a Waffen SS uniform. There are many good books on the market, particularly

The base colour consists of two tones of green.

Osprey's Warrior 2, Men at Arms 34 and 234, Elite 11 and Campaign series 1 and 24.

Once the colours, forms and details have been studied, start by applying the base colour, which usually consists of two light tones. The camouflage design will be painted on top of this. In the case illustrated, the base colour (a light green tone with grey undertones) was obtained by mixing olive green, cadmium yellow, gold and grey

(using Vallejo Film Color acrylics). To lighten, add grey to the base mix, keeping in mind that this part of the painting process will differ from the usual in that only one light coat will be applied. For the most part this coat will be covered by the subsequent painting of camouflage markings.

The next step is painting the colour patterns that make up the camouflage. It is easiest to start with the light colours, in this

The trousers are not camouflaged, so they can be lightened. It took six coats to achieve the right effect.

When painting the green splotches, use a very fine brush stroke.

To lighten the jacket, apply only two coats of the lighter tone.

Let the base colour show at the edge when lightening the brown splotches.

There is a noticeable difference between the light areas of the coat and the light areas of the trousers.

COLOUR TABLE

Colour base
Base: Olive green (a-77) + cadmium yellow (c-22) + grey (a-2)
Highlights: Base + grey (a-2)

Light camouflage
Base: Burnt sienna (a-91) + beige (b-17)
Highlights: Base + beige (b-17)

Dark camouflage
Base: Dark olive (b-78)
Highlights: Base + grey (a-2)

Shadows
A dark neutral colour

(References are to Vallejo's colour ranges)

The first splotch of colour should be slightly dark.

case a brownish-red, with pinkish undertones, which can be achieved by mixing burnt sienna with a touch of beige. Using a sable brush (a No 1 would be ideal) with a well-kept tip, paint over the figure, paying close attention to the photos or drawings used as reference.

Once finished, add beige to the base mix to apply diffused lighting in the lower part of each splotch to accentuate the contrast. This process should be repeated throughout the entire camouflage pattern. The next colour is a dark green which does not need to be a mix, simply use the Vallejo dark olive colour and add a touch of grey to lighten. Finally, using brown and green paint the various details (clothing and seams), and lighten wherever necessary.

The final step is shading. The approach here is fairly general, as any attempt to darken each colour individually would result in an excessively complicated task with unsatisfactory results.

The base colour of the coat and trousers is a combination of olive green, cadmium yellow, gold and grey; depending on the proportion of colours applied, a more or less intense tone will be obtained.

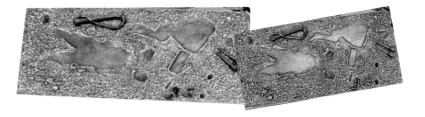

When dry, apply light brown with a dry brush; the weapons can be covered with gunmetal or graphite combined with black paint.

The ground was painted using light brown paint washed over with oil paint.

The lightest colour should cover the highest part of the crease.

The shading tone (which must be very diluted) should be dark and neutral, like the one obtained, for instance, when mixing green, brown and a bit of black. Apply the usual colours and techniques when working on the rest of the bits and pieces. The ground surface is painted with a base colour of light brown. When dry, apply an oil paint wash of dark brown

This figure, in which the brushwork and distribution of splotches can be clearly seen, has undergone ten successive applications of lighter tones.

and red tones. Once the oil paint is dry, lighten using the dry-brush technique, and add suitable ground surface details.

The brown spots follow the form of the fabric creases and are appropriately lightened.

The green outlines the brown splotches.

Within the green splotches, add other lighter spots.

THE BATTLE OF THE BULGE

On 16 September 1944, Hitler interrupted a General Staff meeting to announce what would prove to be his last attack on the Western Front — the Ardennes Offensive.

FIGURES

The figures represent German soldiers belonging to different units; both are of excellent quality and required very few modifications. The Hornet figure is an officer from III/2 (3rd Company, 2nd Regiment) SS Panzergrenadier Regiment, which was part of Kampfgruppe

The primary objective of this ambitious operation was to reach Antwerp and to punch a corridor between the British and American armies. The attack was planned to take place in winter in poor weather conditions, thus neutralising the overwhelming air superiority of the Allied forces.

To paint the officer's leather jacket, apply Decorfin acrylics for the base colour; these will give a satin-like texture.

Small accessories add a sense of completion to the scene.

A technique combining dry-brush and oil wash was used to paint this small piece of cabin.

As well as the green and brown areas, the camouflage design of this three-quarter length jacket is also made up of small dark lines.

TERRAIN

In both cases, creating the surrounding environment is important to the overall atmosphere, but simple to produce. The wood cabin was made using balsa wood and decorated using a mixed technique of acrylic dry brush and oil paint wash. The base colour can consist of any dark brown tone, subsequently lightened with a brownish-yellow (a-85), chalk ochre (b-18), grey (a-2), etc.

This stone wall is from the Miniaturas Ros catalogue. The area of debris was painted with a base of coffee brown (a-82) mixed with a little black. To lighten the grey, apply a chalk ochre (b-18), beige and white. The bricks are a burnt sienna (a-91) and can be lightened with beige (b-17). The snow is a simple mix of baking soda and salt (see also pages 54-55).

'Peiper', the spearhead of the offensive. The officer is wearing a leather jacket and reversible camouflage trousers. The other figure is from the Miniaturas Andrea collection, and is in a 5th Fallschirmjäger Division uniform; note the blue Luftwaffe coat and the weapon — a Stg44 assault rifle.

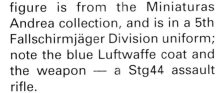

The stone wall is a Miniaturas Ros product.

The base tone of the jacket is a light grey (a-2) mixed with a touch of olive green (a-77).

COLOUR TABLE

Panzergrenadier officer

Coat
Base: Black and sienna (411 Decorfin), coffee brown (a-82)
Highlighting: Sienna (411 Decorfin), burnt sienna (a-91)
Final light coat: Burnt sienna (a-91)

Trousers
Base: Chalk ochre (b-18), coffee brown (a-82)
Highlighting: Beige (b-17)

Fallschirmjäger
Base: Grey (a-2), olive green (a-77)
Highlighting: Grey (a-2) or white (a-90)
Brown spots: Coffee brown (a-82) - to lighten apply burnt sienna (a-91)
Green spots: Dark olive green (b-76) — to lighten apply olive green (a-77)

(Vallejo colour references)

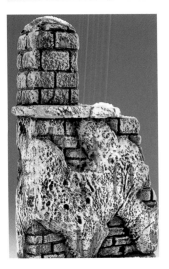

GERMAN FALLSCHIRMJÄGER — 1

The German army was not the first to make successful use of paratroops; well before Germany, countries such as Italy and Russia had used the enormous offensive potential offered by airborne attackers.

After witnessing the impressive results of paratroops in the Soviet Union, Hermann Goering was put in charge of creating the first German Fallschirmjäger units. The initial offensives by the German paras were in Norway and Denmark. Here we recreate two very different theatres in which the troops were involved — Crete and Cassino.

FIGURES

The first figure is an officer from the Luftlande-Sturm-Regiment preparing to fly to the island of Crete in May 1941, as part of Operation '*Merkur*' (mercury), as the airborne invasion was codenamed. This top quality figure is in the Miniaturas Andrea catalogue (ref. S5-F20). It was slightly improved with the addition of the MP40 cartridges, which paras attached to their legs to avoid them snagging in the 'chute cords during jumps.

The other figure is in the same range (ref. S5-F13), and is an officer belonging to the 1st Fallschirmjäger Division, which between the months of January and May took part in one of the unit's most heroic operations, the defence of Monte Cassino

The para's battledress smock has a complicated camouflage pattern.

A different torso was adapted to fit this figure, and extra detail was added to the helmet.

The hand holding the machine gun was modelled with putty.

monastery. For this figure the head has been substituted for another manufactured by Hornet. The left hand was removed and a new one modelled using putty to fit the FG42 machine gun better. The helmet straps were also custom-made to look more realistic; similarly the sleeve patches were modelled with putty.

TERRAIN

The grass is simple to make. One of the sections was made by taking a small piece of turf and lightly painting over it with a dry brush and yellow paint. To suggest the bombed-out environment of Cassino and an element of devastation, the

acrylics was applied; this was subsequently worked over with lighter tones and touches of wash using black and burnt sienna oil paint.

This back view of the figure shows the extensive detailing of the parachute.

COLOUR TABLE

Jump smock
Base: Grey (a-2) + bluish-grey (b-68) + olive-green (a-77)
Highlighting: Base + bluish-grey (b-68) + white

Camouflaged jump smock
Base: olive grey (a-94) + grey (a-2) + white
Highlighting: base + white

Camouflage markings
Base: Olive green (a-77)
Highlighting: Olive green (a-77) + burnt sienna (a-91) + beige (b-17)
Base: Burnt sienna (a-91)
Highlighting: Burnt sienna (a-91) + beige (b-17)

A few simple accessories are enough to create a realistic atmosphere around the figure.

figure stands in front of a damaged stone wall. With the exception of some retouching and the addition of some minor elements, this wall from the Verlinden catalogue was not changed significantly. To colour the wall, a primary coat of dark

The cartridge clips for the machine gun are attached to the lower section of the trousers.

GERMAN FALLSCHIRMJÄGER — 2

During the last year of the war in Europe, German parachute troops played an active role on all fronts, but mainly as ground troops.

As the war progressed, attrition saw the majority of the original parachute division personnel wiped out, and few occasions to use their primary skills. Apart from a small drop during the Ardennes campaign (see below), they were used as ground infantry. They fought with distinction wherever they were used — for example, Ramcke's 2FJD (2nd Fallschirmjäger Division) would hold out in Brest until September 1944, when US troops were within a hundred metres of his command post. Many of the unit remnants from the long defensive battles in Normandy and Italy were reorganised into new units using ad hoc personnel — many being Luftwaffe ground troops — who would keep on fighting until the bitter end.

FIGURES

The two figures shown in this article are high quality figures belonging to the Miniaturas Andrea catalogue. They complement the two previous figures and are part of our collection of German paratroops from World War II.

One of the figures (S5F33) shows an NCO of 2FJD, based in Brittany and, latterly, Brest until it surrendered. (A reconstituted 2FJD was raised in Holland in December 1944.) The only feature distinguishing these parachute troops from regular infantry was the fact that the Fallschirmjäger retained the old olive-green coat used when jumping. A head produced by Hornet replaced this figure's original one, and a set of badges (photo-etched on metal by Nimex) were added.

The second figure (ref.

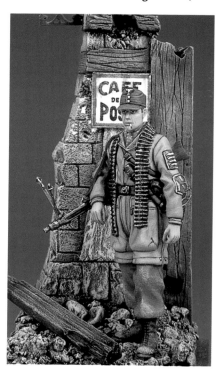

S5F29) is a Fallschirmjäger Regiment 6 (FJR6) soldier who took part in what was probably the last mission that these troops engaged in as para-troops. It took place during the Ardennes Offensive when a small contingent was dropped near the Malmedy–Eupen road, in an attempt to cut the supply lines of the Allied forces in the area. This figure was improved by adding various details.

TERRAIN

To set off the two paratroopers we have created small but striking environments around the figures. The first element used to create the scene was a piece of wall (from Verlinden Productions), which was painted using a mixed technique of oils and acrylics.

The second stage was to add natural elements such as twigs and bristles. Then, to simulate snow, baking soda and salt were scattered over the scene.

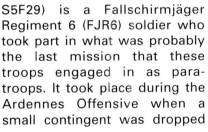

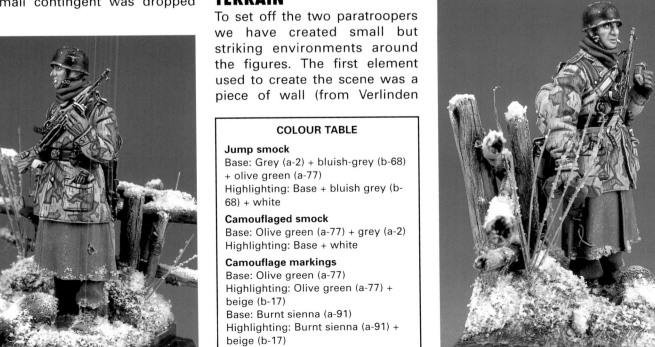

COLOUR TABLE
Jump smock
Base: Grey (a-2) + bluish-grey (b-68) + olive green (a-77)
Highlighting: Base + bluish grey (b-68) + white
Camouflaged smock
Base: Olive green (a-77) + grey (a-2)
Highlighting: Base + white
Camouflage markings
Base: Olive green (a-77)
Highlighting: Olive green (a-77) + beige (b-17)
Base: Burnt sienna (a-91)
Highlighting: Burnt sienna (a-91) + beige (b-17)

GERMAN FALLSCHIRMJÄGER — 3

The Fallschirmjäger played a fundamental role as an elite corps within the German Armed Forces.

During the early days of Blitzkrieg, in Norway, Denmark, Holland and Belgium, the Fallschirmjäger were at the forefront of the German Armed Forces. They gained fame for neutralising

---

COLOUR TABLE
(OFFICER)

Shirt
Base: Brownish-yellow (a-85) +ochre (b-18) + beige (917)
Highlighting: Base + beige (917) + white (951)
Shading: Umber (a-92).

Shorts
Base: Beige (917) + ochre green cadmium (c-82) + olive grey (a-94)
Highlighting: Base + white (951)
Shading: Umber (a-92)

(References are to Vallejo's Model Color and Film Color range)

Because this figure is in a North African environment his skin should be tanned.

There is a subtle tonal difference between the shirt and trousers.

strategic locations in the pathway of the advancing Panzers — bridges, airfields, forts, such as the classic action in capturing Eben Emael fort in Holland.

In the Mediterranean the Fallschirmjäger were particularly successful, capturing the Corinth canal in Greece, attacking the island of Crete (Operation 'Merkur') and taking part in the campaign in Tunisia. The Führer was reluctant, however, to use these troops as airborne units after Crete

Using an ochre-green colour, grime has been suggested at the bottom of the trousers and on the helmet.

because, despite holding back British forces in the area, the operation took its toll on the Germans after heavy fighting against the New Zealand Brigade.

Later, in 1943, some parachute units were deployed on the Smolensk Front in the Ukraine.

FIGURES

The first figure is made by English manufacturer Hornet, and is of exceptional quality. Nevertheless this piece has gone through a complex transformation process to represent a I/FJR5 officer from the Tunisian campaign.

The second figure is made by the Spanish manufacturer, La Compañia. This piece was also changed by placing it in the Russian snows during the winter of 1942–43. The head on the figure is also a Hornet piece.

TERRAIN

The surroundings developed for both figures are fairly simple. The vegetation consists of small branches and natural grass. To make the ground we followed the usual dry brush and oil wash techniques. The small wall in the Russian scene can be found in the Miniaturas Alemany catalogue.

COLOUR TABLE
(FALLSCHIRMJÄGER)

Jump smock
Base: Military green (975) + dark grey (994) + matt yellow (953) + pale grey (990)
Highlighting: Base + silver grey (883)
Shading: Base + German grey (995)

Trousers
Base: White (951) + brown (986) + light yellow (949)
Highlighting: Base + white (951)
Shading: Navy grey (991)

(References are to Vallejo's Model Color and Film Color range)

The base colour of the blouse is a mix of grey, yellow and green.

DEUTSCHES AFRIKA KORPS — 2

German military intervention in North Africa came as a direct consequence of the heavy losses suffered by the Italian forces in Egypt and Libya.

aid offered by the Germans. After suffering heavy losses in Sidi Barrani, Bardia and Beda Fomm, at which the Italians lost 130,000 men and 380 tanks, German military support became an unwelcome necessity, as has been discussed earlier in this book.

Once the Germans arrived in Africa, the Commonwealth troops — consisting of soldiers from Britain, Australia, India and New Zealand — had to confront a very different type of army.

FIGURES

The two figures included in this work belong to the catalogues of Spanish manufacturers and their quality is second to none.

The first figure is a Panzer Pioneer (engineer) of the Miniaturas Andrea collection (ref. S5-F10) and is made of metal. The Panzer engineers were elite units, used as shock troops to clear the way for the main infantry assault; their weaponry, therefore, was heavy on hand grenades (seen slung in pouches) and all manner of automatic weapons.

The other is a resin figure made by the Zaragoza firm, La Compañia (ref. 35-204), and shows a high-ranking German officer. In a continuing effort to make their clothing more suitable and comfortable for desert conditions — very hot by day, surprisingly cold by night — the DAK troops modified their issue clothing with a variety of changes during the course of the campaign. In the early stages, the German lack of tropical

B efore these setbacks, however, Hitler had already offered assistance in the form of a Panzer division, but prior to the invasion of Egypt Mussolini rejected any form of

experience meant that many items of equipment shipped to Africa were inappropriate, and many of the officers continued wearing the uniform they used in the European theatre.

COLOUR TABLE

Army jacket (both figures)
Base: Ochre green (c-89) + dark olive (b-78)
Highlighting: Base + ochre green (c-89) + beige
Shading: Base + black

Trousers (Panzer Pioneer)
Base: Ochre green (c-89) + olive green (a-77)
Highlighting: Umber (a-92)

Trousers (Officer)
Base: Ochre green (c-89) + beige
Highlighting: Base + beige and white

TERRAIN

In order to create a suitable environment to show off the model, a small piece of terrain has been made for each figure. The two bits of desert are quite similar and fairly simple to make. Using a wooden surface, model a base of putty over which sand and small pieces of stone can be scattered (to stick them, use white glue diluted with water). The sandbags were also modelled using putty; some were made to look as if they had been torn, and a coating of fine sand was added for realism. To paint the ground surface, use the usual techniques for acrylics: over the base colour, apply gentle dry brush work and successive diluted coats of oil paint to emphasise areas of relief.

NORMANDY 1944

German armoured units and British Commandos played important roles on opposite sides of the Battle of Normandy.

The figures are currently presented in two sets: 'Spanish in the Second World War' and 'Normandy', from the latter of which these two figures belong; their references are 35201 'Oficial Carrista SS' and 35202 'Comando Britanico'.

A relatively new Spanish model-making company, La Compañia, has recently released five top quality metal figures onto the market. All are modelled by Diego F. Fortes, and are accurately reproduced at a scale of 1/35, which not only makes them attractive collectables, but also makes them ideal to complement military vehicles and dioramas.

A preliminary coat of filler will show up any assembly flaws and highlight the details of the figure.

The first step is to apply the initial coat of paint to the uniform using a mix of bluish-grey and olive green.

Start to lighten by applying a mixture of the base colour and grey (a-2).

Begin painting the yellow spots over the base colour with a mixture of ochre green and yellow.

To paint the brown splotches apply burnt sienna, slightly darkened with black.

The colours used to imitate the camouflage design should complement the base colour.

PREPARATION AND ASSEMBLY

To clean and prepare these pieces we used a modelling knife and fine sandpaper. The pieces were cemented together with cyanoacrylate adhesive, and to fill cracks and cover mistakes, putty was applied. For the British Commando, the most difficult elements to model were the automatic rifle belt and the two straps of the backpack. To make them realistic we used strips of tin cut to size, a small clothes peg and plenty of patience.

PAINTING

Use the same flesh colour for both figures; base colour is brownish-gold (a-86), white (a-90) and dark yellow (202 Decorfin). To lighten, mix white (100 Decorfin); for shading, use a diluted burnt sienna (a-91).

The German officer comes from the 12th SS Panzer Division 'Hitlerjugend', which on D-Day was to be found west of Caen,

The shading and outlining of the figure help to define the form and details over the dominant camouflage pattern.

Elements such as details on the cap need to be carefully outlined.

defending against the Allied advance: it would be decimated in the Falaise pocket.

The most striking feature of this piece is the uniform, which is accurately rendered in an

The Obersturmführer's badge has a dark green background colour with stripes and leaves in a light grass green tone.

Italian fabric. The greyish-green used as the base colour is obtained by mixing bluish-grey (b-68), olive-green (a-77) and grey (a-2), this last colour will be used to lighten the finished article. The yellowish-coloured splotches are ochre green cadmium (c-89), lightened with yellow, and the brown splotches are burnt sienna, darkened with a bit of black. To finish, apply some general shading using a

The leather tone of the holster and boots has a base colour of black (700 Decorfin).

diluted black. The SS Obersturmführer's badge has a background colour of dark green with decorative elements in the form of stripes and leaves in a light grass green.

The British soldier could belong to any Commando unit which was part of either the 1st or 4th Special Forces Brigade as both disembarked at Normandy. The main objective of these elite units was the occupation of strategic points behind enemy lines, to secure and protect the flanks during the Allied advance.

To get the uniform's brownish-grey khaki colour, blend light brown (a-83), cadmium ochre green (c-89) and coffee brown (a-82); to lighten, apply cadmium ochre green and a little bit of beige.

Begin by applying a preliminary coat of ochre green, coffee brown and light brown.

The base colour used for painting the areas of flesh is a blend of Decorfin golden brown, white and dark yellow.

The most interesting part of Commando's equipment is his assault jerkin — something that did not see much wartime service. Originally designed by Colonel Rivers MacPherson, RAOC, some 19,000 were distributed to assault troops of 21st Army Group before the D-Day landings. The jerkin varied in colour depending on theatre of use. In Europe they were dark brown. To get the correct colour, the base is a mix of chocolate (a-88), coffee brown (a-82) and a bit of black.

Over the base colour of the uniform, apply the lighter coats using ochre green, cadmium and beige.

The shading and outlining of forms and details are painted using a mix of the base colour and umber.

To lighten, progressively apply burnt sienna.

For much of the time, Commandos did not wear their metal helmets preferring the green beret — the symbol of their special status. The particular colour of this item can be imitated using green (b-80) plus touches of Prussian blue and burnt olive.

The pack is painted in a canvas colour obtained by mixing yellowish-brown (a-85), olive green (a-77) and umber (a-92); to lighten, apply brown, yellow and beige.

The belts have a base of cadmium ochre green (c-89) and beige (b-17) with a bit of umber; this can be lightened using beige or white.

Begin painting the vest using coffee brown, slightly darkened with black.

Emphasise the stitching on the vest with a beige colour.

The belt and gaiters have a base colour of greenish-ochre, cadmium, beige, plus a touch of umber.

The sleeve emblem was hand-painted using dark blue and red. The white lettering was added later.

The colour of the backpack is made by mixing yellowish-brown, olive green and umber.

The right shade of beret can be obtained by blending green, plus touches of Prussian blue and burnt olive.

The khaki colour used by the British was predominantly ochre and brown instead of the usual green.

COLOUR TABLE
(References are to Vallejo's Film Color range)

German officer
Italian camouflage
Base: Greyish-blue (b-68)
   + olive green (a-77)
   + grey (a-2)
Highlighting: Base + grey (a-2)
Shading: Diluted neutral colour
Light spots: Cadmium ochre
   green (c-89) + yellow (c-22)
Dark spots: Burnt sienna
   (a-91) + a bit of black

Commando
Uniform:
Base: Cadmium ochre green (c-89) + coffee
   brown (a-82) + light brown (a-83)
Highlighting: Base + c-89 and beige
Shading: Base + umber (a-92)
Vest:
Base: Chocolate brown (a-88) + coffee
   brown (a-82) + black
Highlighting: Base + burnt sienna (a-91)
Shading: Base + black

WAFFEN SS PANZER UNITS

On 18 July 1944, just south of Caen, Operation 'Goodwood' started — Montgomery's attempt to break out from the Normandy bridgehead.

This controversial operation was preceded by heavy' Allied bombing of German positions — something that would see much of historic Caen and other locations devastated. To begin with, all seemed well as three tank divisions attacked and the British armoured units achieved their primary objectives. But as the Allies continued their advance, the German response was launched: they stopped the Allies cold with the Panzers of 1st SS Panzer Division 'Leibstandarte Adolf Hitler' (LSSAH) in the fore. The next day elements from the Hitlerjugend and 'Hohenstaufen' divisions joined the LSSAH and the advance bogged down. In the long run, however, it had weakened other areas of the German defence and shortly afterwards Patton's Third (US) Army was able to go onto the offensive.

COLOUR TABLE

Coat
Base: Black.
Highlighting: Black, grey (a-2).

Trousers
Base: Natural shade (a-92)
Light spots: Cadmium red (c-42), beige (b-17)
Light spots: Green (b-75), white
Dark spots: Olive (b-78)
Dark spots: Coffee brown (a-82)

Camouflage overalls
Base: Burnt sienna (a-91), beige (b-17)
Dark spots: Olive (b-78)
Light spots: Green (a-77), white

(References are to Vallejo's colour ranges)

FIGURES

The first figure is from the Miniaturas Andrea catalogue (ref. S5-F5) and is of excellent quality, although we replaced the head with one from a Hornet figure. Apart from this, no other significant transformations were made to the SS-Untersturmführer of LSSAH's Panzer Regiment 1. The short coat and camouflage trousers are typical of the uniform worn by German soldiers during the final stages of the war.

The other figure is made of resin and manufactured by Hornet. The figure represents an officer of a reconnaissance unit belonging to the 9th SS Panzer Division 'Hohenstaufen'. In this case the officer is found wearing camouflage coveralls of the 'oak leaf' type, commonly used by the Waffen SS in Normandy.

TERRAIN

The ground for both pieces is quite similar so the same processes will be used for creating the two. First, model the terrain over the base and then

add elements such as rocks. The pieces are painted using a darkish base tone, preferably a coffee brown mixed with black or Prussian blue; lighten with a dry brush using various tones of ochre or beige, but always working from dark to light.

Finally, add vegetation, over which a wash of oil paint or a final touch of dry brush is applied to reduce shine. An oil paint wash is also an effective way of hiding any areas showing excess paint.

SS 'HANDSCHAR' DIVISION

On 1 March 1943, Hitler ordered the formation of the 13th Waffen-Gebirgs-Division der SS, a division made up entirely of volunteers from the Muslim Croat population.

engagements in the Balkans. At first, the high number of volunteers made forced recruitment unnecessary, but later on conscription became mandatory.

The 13th Division was named 'Handschar' and attached to the 5th Mountain Corps of the Waffen SS. It saw action during 1944, carrying out operations against Serb guerrilla forces.

In June 1944 a second Muslim division was established, the 23rd Waffen Gebirgs-Division der SS 'Kama' was made up of some 9,000 men, but was never completely operational and

was dissolved in the autumn of that same year.

FIGURES

The two soldiers shown here were made by different manufacturers, and both require work in order to make the uniforms adapt to the figures.

The first figure is an SS Hauptsturmführer of the 'Handschar' Division from the Miniaturas Andrea collection. This high-quality figure is perfect for the kind of modifications that are required. The only changes made were the sanding down of some extraneous details and the replacement of the head with one made by Hornet.

The environment around this figure primarily consists of a section of wall; also included is a piece of etched-brass iron railing and artificial vegetation.

Because of the history of the Balkans, these troops felt particular hatred toward the Christian Serbs who made up Tito's partisans — nothing changes: these hatreds caused World War I and the recent

The painting is fairly straightforward, helped by the fact that both uniforms utilise simple colours. The most complicated part is acquiring accurate uniform reference in the first place, and outlining the officer's anorak.

TERRAIN

Making the terrain is simple, although the size of the base surface may add an element of

The other figure represents a second officer from the same unit, this time equipped with a campaign uniform. It is a Hecker and Goros piece which, although it looks good alongside other pieces, cannot be compared with the first figure in terms of quality. This piece has also been slightly changed and also has a new head provided by Hornet.

This officer wearing a campaign outfit is a Hecker and Goros piece. Although the quality is acceptable, it was necessary to improve certain features.

COLOUR TABLE

(References are to Vallejo's colour ranges)

Grey uniform
Base: Grey (a-2) + black + olive green (a-77) + royal blue (b-61)
Highlighting: Base + grey (a-2) + white
Shading: Base + black

Anorak
Base: Grey (a-2) + white + a little yellow
Highlighting: Base + white
Shading: Base + grey

difficulty to the task. The Minituras Andreas officer figure is placed next to a section of wall (from Verlinden). The base colour is coffee brown (a-82) and Prussian blue (b-60), lightened by applying various tones of ochres and browns with a dry brush, and a final wash of oil paint using black and burnt sienna. The other figure is on a natural base.

SS POLIZEI-GRENADIER

At the end of 1945, the German Army concentrated most of its forces against the Soviet advance, in the hope that most of Germany would be occupied by western armies.

lacking the number of men required to form a regiment.

The figure in the vignette represents one of these police units: specifically, a Scharführer (sergeant) from the SS Polizei-Grenadier Division. Formed in February 1945, this division fought on the Niesse Front and surrendered to the Soviets in Halbe, east of Prague, in May of that same year. He displays a combination of Waffen SS camouflage clothing and the M44 short coat.

FIGURE

The figure is made by Hornet (ref. GH-6) and the quality, as is always the case with this manufacturer's work, is excellent. To make this police sergeant, we started with minor changes,

adding the belt and medals which Verlinden sells in the form of etched-brass accessories.

The painting techniques used on the camouflage areas of the uniform are the same as those discussed elsewhere in this book. It is worth noting, however, that the camouflage pattern covering the trousers is of the 'pea' type, used after 1943 by the Waffen SS, and the pattern found on the helmet covering is of the 'oak leaf' type.

TERRAIN

The façade of the house is made of balsa wood and the door is made of strips of the type used

Lack of resources forced the Germans to use police units as combat troops. Although they were referred to as divisions, these units were poorly equipped, as well as often

This façade is made with balsa wood then covered with putty to simulate an authentic texture. The signs are from Verlinden.

The door is made of small strips of wood and the windows can be made from plastic or acetate.

To paint the ground surface of the vignette and to emphasise details use both the wash and dry brush methods.

in naval modelling. The debris, was made from Das Pronto putty. The signs are from Verlinden and the windows are made of transparent plastic.

The door was given a base tone made up of olive and black, which was lightened using grey (a-2). The preliminary coat used for the façade was a mixture of coffee brown (a-82) with black, which was later lightened with ochre and beige by using a dry brush. To finish a wash of black was applied. All the colour references are from Vallejo.

The quality of this Hornet figure is excellent, although the piece can be enhanced by adding medals and Verlinden etched-brass accessories.

'AUF WIEDERSEHEN ITALY'

The German defence of Italy in 1944–45 exemplified the strengths of their armed forces. In spite of Allied air superiority, the disparity of troop numbers and a dearth of supplies, the 'soft underbelly' of the Axis did not give way.

Far from it. Thanks to an intelligent use of their limited resources, the Germans were able to resist the Allied advance right up until the unconditional surrender of their forces in Italy on 2 May 1945.

After Rome was declared an open city on 4 June 1944, the Germans organised several lines of defence in Orvieto and the Arno Valley in an effort to slow the Allied advance towards Florence, which eventually fell on 12 August. By that time, the Germans had developed the Gothic Line, which maintained strongpoints in the mountains, defended access routes to Bologna and Ravenna.

Nevertheless, Rimini fell to the Allies on 2 September, Forli on 10 November and Ravenna on 15 December. By the end of the year, the Allies came to a standstill along the Senio river and the Italian Front remained static throughout the winter.

Fighting intensified in the spring when the US Fifth and

British Eighth Armies breached the enemy lines on either side of Bologna and linked up in the Po Valley, just days before the end of the war.

Both sides suffered in the final winter of the war: the Allies having lost men and material to the Western Front, the Germans severely hampered by lack of supplies.

German troops stationed in northern Italy presented little uniformity in terms of clothing. It was common for the Wehrmacht and Waffen SS to be equipped with a haphazard combination of the usual Feldgrau uniforms, Luftwaffe clothing, Italian material, camouflage outfits and tropical garments. We have attempted to reflect the casual nature of the troops' clothing in this vignette.

TERRAIN

This scene could have taken place at any number of locations in northern Italy just days before the surrender of the German forces. The scenario is that of a small Waffen SS detachment of two soldiers waiting to be taken captive by Allied troops and only too well aware that Germany had lost the war.

The ground surface is made with modelling filler. The ground is painted with Matt 88 from Revell, then lightened by adding a white tone to this colour and applying with a dry brush. The grass is an Aneste product painted with Vallejo green tones.

The tent is made from four ponchos which fitted together in a pyramid shape. Made from rubberised cloth, each soldier received a shelter quarter for use as illustrated or as an individual poncho — this accounts for the apparent discrepancy of colour shown by the shelter, with one side displaying the camouflage pattern and the other a cream-coloured fabric.

To model this structure we used an Italeri tent, from the Kübelwagen 1/35 kit. Its quality left a lot to be desired, but was acceptable as a foundation piece over which details could be added. The entrance was made from a tin sheet; the buttoned areas linking the ponchos together were reworked with small strips of plastic and small cuts made with a blade to simulate buttonholes. The camouflage pattern is of a well-known geometric type; the non-camouflaged side was painted with a mix of Vallejo acrylics, using brownish-yellow (a-85) and white.

The corrugated barrels were made from tin sheet, stretched with a pen and curved; the circular plastic lids were added later and the fuel cap openings were made using copper wire. The jerry cans were made in the same way. The other barrels are made by Verlinden.

When painting the medicine boxes and the stool, special attention was given to the rendering of the wood grain, which was obtained with an umber base mixed with a brownish-yellow and white.

The metal container was built in the same way as the barrels, but with fine wire handles. The 10-litre carrier at the front of the

tent was made by sanding down a piece of resin until the desired shape was reached; handles and

clasps were made of wire. Both the container and the barrel were painted in a sandy tone and aged by an umber wash.

The signposts were computer generated, printed on paper then glued on to a thin sheet of plastic. The signs were laminated and then aged by going over with a fine piece of sandpaper and finally washing with umber and black.

FIGURES

The Obersturmführer (in shorts) is a Miniaturas Andrea figure. This high-quality figure is cast in lead, the modelling outstanding, resulting in a very natural and realistic posture. Thanks to an excellent sculpting job, the task of painting over the shapes is fairly easy and a sense of realism is easily achieved as long as the direction of the light source is considered when shading and highlighting.

No changes were made at all to this figure which was painted to the manufacturer's guidelines. The soldier's appearance clearly shows the eclectic mix of clothing available by this stage of the war. The army jacket is typically coloured and would have been made to measure by the regimental tailor; the sandy yellow shorts are probably of Italian origin and in a tone slightly darker than the cap; the mountain boots have typically spiked soles; the socks are also Feldgrau and the tropical cap is a 1943 model, of a light sandy yellow tone. An SS eagle was painted in lemon yellow (c-21) and brownish-yellow (a-85) on the cap. The Totenkopf (skull and crossbones insignia) is painted in a Titan gold enamel.

The SS Scharführer is a Verlinden piece (ref. 644), and needed minor modifications. The cape is of the tropical kind, coloured in olive green, and has been elongated at the bottom by adding tin foil cemented with Tamiya putty. The head was replaced by another, of the same make but with a different expression, and the sandy coloured cap was modelled out of putty, with the peak made from tin. The epaulets, emblem and Luftwaffe scarf are the same colour as the eagle motif on the officer's cap. The binoculars actually belong to the other figure and are made in resin from a silicone cast, then painted in a sandy tone. The boots and the belt are the same colour as the officer's footwear. The belt on the metal tube is painted in a green tone, slightly lighter than the cape, and the Luger holster is in satin black.

SKI-JÄGER BRIGADE

Right from the start, when they began operating in 1915, the mountain hunters of the Ski-Jäger were recognised as elite units of the German Army.

The Anchluss in 1938 integrated the old Austrian Army, including its crack hunter-skier troops, into the Wehrmacht. These experienced mountain units were rigorously trained in high terrain combat and followed a strong alpine tradition. Thanks to their specialised abilities, the Austrians greatly enhanced the operational capacity of the German Gebirgsjäger divisions — a combination that had fought together previously during World War I, when the two nations battled against Italian forces in the Alps.

In Germany, three ski battalions raised in Bavaria in 1915 formed the 3rd Jäger Regiment in the Alpine Corps that served in Serbia, on the Western Front and in the Carpathians; the Württemberg Ski Battalion fought in the Vosges, Transylvania and Italy.

During World War II, after emphatic interventions in Poland, Norway, the Balkans, Greece and the island of Crete, the mountain divisions confronted the Soviets on the South-Eastern Front. On this front, Nazi forces took the Caucasus mountains and even reached the peak of Mount Elbruz at a height of 5,633m.

This diorama shows action taking place during the winter of 1943, in the Norwegian-Finnish theatre. The scene is that of a Ski-jäger reconnaissance unit, surprised by enemy fire in Lapland. Considering the unpredictable weather conditions, hostile temperatures and potential enemy attacks, the Germans would have suffered far greater losses if not for the experience and resistance of the Gebirgsjäger troops.

FIGURES

The skis, poles, caps, backpacks and most of the equipment is common to all of the figures, so, the figure in motion can be taken as our example. The

To make the tree, start with a putty-modelled trunk. The foliage canopy is created with small pieces of real branches and artificial moss.

descending skier is made of resin and is in the Warriors catalogue. It is of excellent quality with outstanding clothing and equipment. Thanks to very careful sculpting, the posture of the figure is extremely dynamic and provides a dramatic sense of movement and excitement to the scene.

During the assembly of this figure, the skis were replaced by another set from the Dragon German Ski-troopers kit; the attachments were improved by using copper wire and tin sheet. The poles are stretched pieces of plastic, the belts and rings at the end of the poles are made of wire and tin sheet. Using these same materials, laces have been added for the hood, anorak stiffeners and belt buckle. On one of the sides of the cap the metallic emblem of the Ski-jäger (three oak leaves and a diagonal ski) is found, while blizzard goggles were placed over the head of one of the figures — both of these details were made from Duro putty.

The spare magazine pouches for the MP40 have been

The sniper is a plastic figure from the Dragon collection. A new pair of hiking boots were added plus new accessories from Verlinden.

To simulate snow, make a blend of white marble powder and salt, then mix with diluted white glue. Apply fresh, with a palette knife.

This skier is one of Warrior's finest figures.

The base colour of all three figures is a grey tone. This base colour will make the application of lighter tones easier, allowing for a rich variety of lighting and shading effects.

separated one by one to fit better around the waist. The butt of the weapon was remade using wire. Finally, the ubiquitous German steel helmet, painted white, was also added as a piece of equipment. The colour was toned down by washing with black and umber, and fine brush touches were finally added using black and silver. When painting the poles and white skis, this same technique was used but without the final touch of silver paint.

The officer stationed behind the rocks is a resin copy of the previous figure, with some minor changes — the belts were eliminated and pockets for the anorak were added using Duro putty. The position of his arms was modified and adapted to the new posture by heating and twisting; a P-38 pistol was placed in the left hand, while the right hand was replaced by one belonging to a spare figure. The boots were also replaced with a pair made by Verlinden. The head is made by Hornet; the goggles and typical alpine beard were modelled using Duro putty. His skis, unlike those belonging to the other figures, were painted in a wood brown tone (Vallejo acrylic). Attached to the belt is the holster and a pair of gloves modelled using Duro.

The sniper is from the Dragon German Gebirgsjäger kit, with the addition of some equipment pieces and hiking boots from Verlinden. The rest

of this figure's equipment is found on the bottom right side of the diorama to break the otherwise uninteresting white snow surface.

It is during the painting phase that the figures can really be improved; it is important, however, to be specially careful when colouring the white uniforms. Here we opted to work over a base tone of light grey — this colour facilitated the lightening process until pure white was reached. Also, the figures were not outlined in black but in a dark greenish-grey to reduce the tonal contrast.

TERRAIN
After getting the desired slope from a sheet of cork, small stones were added to suggest rock formations. Afterwards, the relief was completed with Das Pronto putty. The rocks were painted with a blend of acrylic black, chocolate brown and yellowish-brown — to lighten add more of the last two colours. To finish, wash with black and umber, and finish with some final touches of chocolate brown and red on a dry brush. To make the tree,

The ski gear gives each figure an interestingly elaborate assortment of accessories.

of Tamiya olive green (XF-62) over the foliage to give a uniformity of colour.

It is always problematic to get snow to scale and looking realistic. After discarding other options, the snow was made by mixing powdered white marble, fine salt and white glue diluted in water. While still fresh, the mix was applied with a palette knife, over the trees and ground surface. The icicles were made by stretching transparent plastic and applying two coats of Marabu glossy varnish.

Finally, it is worth mentioning that modelling this mini diorama at 1/35 scale was a real challenge, particularly the snow. That it was successful was highlighted when it won a silver medal within its category in the latest AMT contest.

begin with a trunk modelled from Milliput; subsequently work in several real branches which will serve to support a variety of leaves. The leaves are made of freeze-dried moss of a type sold for nativity scenes; they should be carefully selected and considered for their form and size. With care this approach will produce a realistic, natural conifer. To finish, airbrush a coat

A detail that should not be forgotten is footprints in the snow!

FRIEND OR FOE? — FRANCE 1944

Judging by the work found in competitions and the material submitted to model-making publications, it is evident that a figure integrated into an environment is becoming an increasingly popular challenge. This is undoubtedly because a good background reinforces the overall finish and enhances the visual impact of the piece.

F riend or foe? Does it belong to the Resistance or is it a collaborator? This is what the doubtful sentry seems to ask himself upon the appearance of a haughty French cockerel — although after days of fighting and army food, the question would more likely be, breast or thigh?

The scene takes place on a French farm, in the months following the invasion of Normandy.

TERRAIN

To start off the construction of the wall we used 'stone house/window' [*casa de piedra/ventana*] from the Spanish company Alemany (ref. 35001). We began by eliminating the gap left for the upper window, by sanding down the surface. Next, all the gaps between the stones were gone over with a burin to bring out the relief.

To build the eave projecting from the roof, a wedge of chalk was placed on the top of the wall, over which a rectangular piece of wood (slightly projecting outwards) was glued. Afterwards, the roof tiles were cut out from strips of plastic card; these were then overlapped and glued in position. Finally, all superfluous material sticking out from the sides was removed and the edges of the wall sanded down. The windows were made with varying sized strips of wood, with etched brass hinges.

Once the wall was finished, it was glued to the base and strips of masking tape were used to mark out the space that the diorama ground surface would occupy. Using putty, a small grass bush was added — this could have been made from either paint brush bristles or coconut fibre.

Because the ground has no major hills, we applied a simple but effective technique to make the surface. This consists of applying a generous coat of white glue, over which a layer of sand is sprinkled (preferably

The collar is darkened with a wash of brown over the cream-coloured base.

Remove the top section and go over the texture of the façade to improve the stonework.

Add a sloping wedge at the top of the wall to make the roof.

The roof tiles are cut out of plastic sheets and laid to overlap each other.

The shutters were made with strips of wood, and the hinges were from etched brass.

The wall attached to the base — masking tape is used to mark out the diorama surface area.

A coat of white glue is laid down and fine sand sprinkled over.

The tufts of grass were planted at the base of the façade.

use fine sand from the beach or of the kind sold for railway modelling). Once this first layer is dry, some areas were made thicker by following the same procedure.

The painting stage began with the wall. To get the base colour, we blended dark grey (994) with a bit of umber (941), which we subsequently darkened with very dilute and random washes in black, coffee brown and ochre. Once the oil paint dried (it should be left for at least a day) highlighting was applied by

using grey (987) and brown (986) with a dry-brush technique.

The roof tiles were painted in red, brown or grey. As with the wall, we darkened the roof by washing with oil paint, and then lightened it using a dry brush. As a final touch, the gaps between the roof tiles were outlined, small cracks drawn and moss rendered using green oil paint.

The window jambs were painted in dark green (970), and lightened with a greyish-green (973). With touches of desert

yellow (977) we imitated chipped wood on the shutters.

The ground was painted in a matt earth (983). To shade, we applied several washes of dark brown then lightened by adding desert yellow (977) to the base colour at the beginning and khaki yellow (976) near the end — always with a dry brush; white was added to the final coat.

The grass can be glued with the help of diluted white glue. Once glued, apply washes of dark green and superficial touches of dry brush in green

The base colour of the façade is a dark grey mixed with burnt umber.

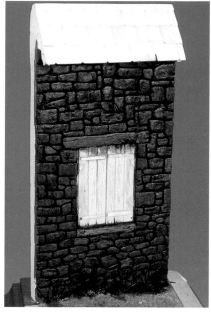

Darken the texture of the wall with a black colour-wash.

Highlight the surfaces using the dry-brush technique.

Paint the different base tones on the roof tiles.

another of the same make — of the head, to get the angle right, and making a rifle sling belt out of a strip of tin. The insignia on the sleeve shows the soldier to be from the 7th Hampshire Regiment, 43rd (Wessex) Division.

Apply cadmium red and light brown over the roof tiles with a dry brush.

Moss is shown by using green oil tones.

tones that are lighter than the base colour.

FIGURE

This piece is Commonwealth Infantryman No 3 (ref. BH-12) from the British firm Hornet. The only modifications made were the replacement — by

To get the khaki brown of the uniform, Vallejo's Model Color English uniform (921) was used, progressively lightened with camouflage yellow (978) plus a bit of khaki yellow (976). The shading colour was created by darkening the base colour with a touch of black, and softly applying this mix in very diluted coats.

The base colour of the belts and gaiters is stone yellow (882)

A final wash will darken and unify the various elements together.

COLOUR TABLE
Terrain
Wall
Base: Dark grey (994) + burnt umber (941)
Highlighting: Base + grey (987) and brown (986)
Shading: Black, brown and ochre (oil)
Tiles
Base: Different tones of red, brown and grey
Highlighting: Light cadmium red (90) + light brown (929)
Shading: Burnt umber and black (oil)
Moss: Green (oil)
Window
Base: Dark green (970)
Highlighting: Base + greenish-grey (973)
Shading: Base + black
Ground
Base: Matt earth (983)
Highlighting: Base + desert yellow (977), khaki yellow (976) and white
Shading: Burnt umber (oil)

Apply base colour to the shutters, then finish with green tones.

The base colour for the ground is a matt earth shade.

Dapple the sand with yellowish-brown tones.

To finish, add tufts of artificial grass in some areas.

How some of the accessories were painted — colours are for the most part wood brown tones.

lightened by careful mixing with white. The helmet is painted in camouflage green (979), with the contrasts made in khaki brown (988) applied with a dry brush; a final light wash in black can be applied at the end if needed. The boots are coloured

The cockerel is the second focal element in the diorama.

Uniform insignia have been painted on with a brush.

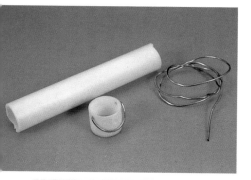

The bucket is made from a plastic tube and wire.

in black (Decorfin 700); to add the effects of dirt, washes of grey (987) and desert yellow were applied.

The metal parts of the rifle were coloured with greasy steel (865) and the wooden parts were painted in brownish-beige (875) and lightened with a golden brown (877).

The cockerel is from the Tamiya farm animal set and was painted in its natural colours using photographic

The success of the entire composition depends on small details such as the placement of the accessories.

references from animal books; the rest of the accessories come from different sources.

The back view shows the personal gear which is painted with a base colour of stone yellow, lightened with white.

COLOUR TABLE
Figure

Uniform
Base: English uniform (921)
Highlighting: Base + white
Shading: Base + chocolate
   brown (872)

Helmet
Base: Camouflage green (979)
Highlighting: Khaki brown (988)
Shading: Very diluted black

Boots
Base: Black (700 Decorfin)
Highlighting: base + dark
   brown (402 Decorfin)
Shading: black

Rifle
Metal: Greasy steel (865)
Wood: Base + beige brown
   (875)
Highlighting: Base + golden
   brown (877)
Shading: Matt brown (984)
   + black

BURMA 1944

Merrill's Marauders was a unit that was specially drawn up for jungle operations in Burma. Its mission was to infiltrate Japanese lines and stir up trouble in the rear.

Many of the men from this unit were veterans who had fought at Guadalcanal and New Guinea. They were chosen for their experience of hostile terrain and their ability to cope with the punishing conditions of jungle warfare.

The unit was made up of three battalions, each of which was divided into combat teams. Each battalion was referred to by colour — red and white for the First Battalion, blue and green for the Second, orange and khaki for the Third.

Each battalion consisted of a command section, a reconnaissance section, an engineer section, a heavy weapons section (which carried three heavy machine guns and four 81mm mortars) and finally a company and a half of infantry.

During their operations in Burma, Merrill's Marauders were extremely successful against the Japanese. One of the unit's most outstanding actions took place around the Numpyek river where, during a five-day period, two Marauder battalions

hounded a much larger group of Japanese forces. The attacks were so devastating that the Japanese lost 800 men, while the Marauders lost only eight dead and 37 wounded.

ASSEMBLY AND PAINTING

The objective with this vignette was to show one of Merrill's Marauders during a mission behind Japanese lines. The soldier advances cautiously through the ruins of a Buddhist temple, virtually covered in dense jungle vegetation.

The back of the shirt is painted mainly in brown and beige tones.

The unshaven face reflects the harrowing pressures of jungle warfare.

The Buddha is a small tourist memento put to a better use than most!

Many of the details of the vegetation are from etched-brass accessories.

In order to give a sense of height and importance to the temple and figure, a balsa wood pedestal was placed over a 5 x 5cm wooden base. Afterwards, the pedestal was covered using epoxy type filler (Milliput, Verlinden, A + B), and when it began to dry, the pedestal and stones underneath the Buddha were carved with an awl.

Once the surfaces were completely dry, painting could begin, using a base mix of coffee brown (a-82), black (a-95) and a bit of Prussian blue (b-60). Subsequently, the base tone was lightened by applying a dry-brush mix of light brown (a-83), cadmium ochre green (c-89), beige (b-17) and a bit of white (a-90); and, later still, by applying a light wash of Rembrandt umber. For the rest of the ground surface, a base colour of light brown (a-83) and a bit of black (a-95) was applied. It was lightened with a dry brush using chocolate brown (a-88), yellowish-brown (a-85), beige (b-17) and a bit of white (a-90). It was finished by applying an oil wash of dark green to the creases.

To show some of the huge variety of jungle vegetation, the plants came from different manufacturers — Verlinden, Scale Link, Nimix — and others were home-made.

To paint the vegetation, a mix of olive green (a-77) and Prussian blue (b-60) was applied, afterwards lightened with olive green (a-77), cadmium golden yellow (c-22) and a bit of white (a-90), and darken with a blend of the base colour and a bit of black (a-95).

The Buddha figure was painted the same way as the temple, emphasising the size and details with a dark green.

The soldier is a well-manufactured and highly-detailed piece from Miniaturas Andrea (ref. S5-F16), and was modelled in a very natural and convincing pose, ideal for the concept on which this vignette is based. Painting this figure took some 25 hours to ensure perfection of the minutest of details, including sweat, dirt and dust, which we felt resulted in as convincing and realistic a model as we have made.

The shirt was painted in a mix of cadmium ochre green (c-89), chocolate brown (a-88) and a bit of beige (b-17), lightened by blending the base colour with grey (a-2) and beige (b-17). The shadows were from a diluted mix of umber (a-92) and black (a-95). The effects of dirt and sweat were made with a diluted mix of burnt sienna (a-91) and golden brown (a-86) in limited areas such as the chest, armpits and back of the figure. The trousers were painted with a base mix of olive green (a-77), umber (a-92), a bit of Prussian blue (b-60) and yellowish brown (a-85), lightened with yellowish-brown (a-85) and beige (b-17), then darkened with burnt olive (b-78) and umber (a-92). All of the colours used to paint

the figure and the surrounding environment are from the Vallejo Film Color acrylic range.

Finally, remember to keep in mind the importance of a good clean presentation, by ensuring the tidy appearance of the base, label and varnish.

This piece was awarded a gold medal in the 1A class, and the Andrea trophy at Euro-militaire, 1992.

GERMANY 1945

During the first days of March 1945, the Allied forces on the Western Front were closing in on Nazi territory, while over on the Eastern Front the Soviets were already fighting on German soil. Before surrendering, the Germans fought desperately, making the Allies pay a high price in human lives.

Slowly, important German cities were occupied by Allied forces — Stuttgart fell on 22 April, then Bremen and Torgau on 27 April. It was in this last city, on the banks of the River Elbe at 16.00 hours, that the 69th Division of the US First Army met the 58th Division of the Soviet Guards of the First Ukrainian Army, thus joining the Eastern and Western Fronts. This event was announced simultaneously in Moscow, London and Washington. Seeing an end to the six-year long war, everyone celebrated joyously.

This diorama shows a Russian woman in the Soviet-occupied River Oder area of Germany. Direction signs were posted throughout the town to help the flow of traffic, supplies and units to the front. To make the directions even clearer, a Russian woman police assistant directs traffic from a street corner.

TERRAIN

The building is made out of plaster, and a chisel was used to render details such as cracks, impacts marks from projectiles, debris and so on. The ruins were placed on a square wooden base, measuring 4 x 4cm.

To paint the ruins, the stucco was coloured with a base mix of brown and golden brown, subsequently lightened by applying a dry brush with yellow plus a bit of white. To show scorch and burn marks, a mix of black and grey was used as a

To paint the figure's shirt use a base mix of burnt olive green and ochre.

These realistic posters and signs are Verlinden accessories.

This building ruin was made out of plaster; details were added by carving with a chisel.

The skirt was lightened progressively with an intense blue and a white.

A wooden surface was used as the base of the vignette — the ground modelled with filler or putty. To paint the ground surface a variety of brown tones were employed.

base, touching over with white on a dry brush. The metal reinforcing rods sticking out of the concrete were made by bending plastic card rods under heat; these were subsequently painted, then metallic reflections added using gun metal and Humbrol silver.

The ground was made from putty, modelled and formed into paving before it dried. To imitate erosion of the stone, a metal-bristled brush was rubbed against the surface until the right texture was obtained. The rubble was also carved from plaster and painted in the same way as the ruins.

To paint the paving, a base mix of Prussian blue and black was used, lightened with grey, ochre and a bit of ivory. The painting stage ended with the application of an English red and umber oil wash to the entire piece.

The posters, signs and accessories were from Verlinden and were used because of their realism and fine finish.

FIGURE

From Hornet, it was to the usual high standards. The shirt and cap were painted with a base mix of burnt olive green and ochre, lightened with grey olive, ochre and a bit of ivory. For the skirt, the base mix was Prussian blue and black, and the item was lightened by

progressively applying an intense blue and white. The boots were painted with a blend of brown and black, and highlighted with a satin finish of Decorfin sienna and yellow.

The rest of the colours were from Vallejo's Film Color range of acrylics.